MEETING WITH MY SELF

SELF-COACHING QUESTIONS THAT INVITE WISDOM IN

GABRIELA CASINEANU

Copyright © 2017 by Gabriela Casineanu

All rights reserved. No portion of this book may be reproduced, distributed, or transmitted in any form or by any means, including photocopying, recording, or other electronic or mechanical methods, without the prior written permission of the author or publisher, except in the case of brief quotations embodied in reviews and certain other noncommercial uses permitted by copyright law.

Although the author and publisher have made every effort to ensure that the information in this book was correct at press time, the author and publisher do not assume and hereby disclaim any liability to any party for any loss, damage, or disruption caused by errors or omissions, whether such errors or omissions result from negligence, accident, or any other cause.

Adherence to all applicable laws and regulations is the sole responsibility of the reader and consumer. Neither the author nor the publisher assumes any responsibility or liability whatsoever on behalf of the consumer or reader of this material. Any perceived slight of any individual or organization is purely unintentional.

Book photos, concept, cover design: Gabriela Casineanu

Cover photo: geralt/pixabay.com

Follow the author:

Facebook: GC.ThoughtsDesigner

Twitter: thoughtdesigner

Instagram: thoughtsdesigner

Website/Blog: GabrielaCasineanu.com

Library and Archives Canada Cataloguing in Publication

Casineanu, Gabriela, 1961—, author

Meeting With My Self: Self-Coaching Questions That Invite the Wisdom In, 1st ed.

ISBN: 978-0-9959677-5-5 (paperback)

ISBN: 978-0-9959677-3-1 (ebook)

CONTENTS

DISCLAIMER

The book *"Meeting With My Self: Self-Coaching Questions That Invite Wisdom In"* invites the reader to engage in self-reflection through a combination of photographs and coaching questions.

This book does not replace counseling, professional coaching, or therapy. The information and resources in this book are provided for informational and educational purposes.

Neither the author nor the publisher can be held responsible for the use of the information provided within this book.

PRAISE FOR THE PHOTO-COACHING BOOK "MEETING WITH MY SELF"

"This is not a book in the traditional sense; it's a tool for communicating with your own inner wisdom.

*I had a chance to use this tool to coach myself through different types of questions — both **personal and professional**. It's been an **amazing tool no matter what question I posed.**"*

~ Rebecca Cuevas

"Among the self-help books that crowd today's marketplace, I found "Meeting with My Self" to be **exceptionally moving and inspirational.**

For me, this book has the deeply moving simplicity of a Japanese Zen garden. In 40 pages, it inspires readers to **explore** their own **unanswered questions in fresh, stimulating ways,** and act on what they discover."

~ E. Thomas Behr

"*I first used this book when I had **lost my job**. At first, I just felt better about myself . Then, as I made it a daily practice and my intention becoming clearer, I began to change the way I thought about my circumstances: **instead of grieving**, I began to **think of the possibilities.***

*I realized I was limiting myself and **I have so much more to offer.** Without having a clear intention each day, all my tasks seemed huge and overwhelming. Now I can focus and accomplish my smaller steps realizing how they are bringing me closer to my goal.*

*This book helped me to **stop whirling around in circles** and to **create a map of where I want my life to go.***"

~Amy Leclercq

❧

"*I really like the picture of the two roads. Before starting my own business, I was **very displeased with my corporate job.** Yet, I couldn't fault my upbringing because I did what I was supposed to: go to school, get good grades, and get a good job.*

*Yet, why was I so dissatisfied? That picture just stood out compared to the rest. My whole life I've been taking the same road as everyone else, while the empty road seemed so inviting, so relaxing, so liberating. **All of my unhappiness melted away**, and I knew which road I had to choose to be happy. Now, regardless of the difficulties I face and the steep learning curves, **all I need to do for motivation is to remember where I was ... and where I want to be.** Thank you!!!*"

Irina P.

❧

"*One page **helped me realize that I was in full transition and transformation** and that there are two parts of my life: the first one full of struggles and the second one more serene ... which **helped me to regain my hope!***"

Natasha Wauthion

PRAISE FOR GABRIELA CASINEANU

"Interesting and somehow impressive was Gabriela's presentation based on this Photo-Coaching book. The contrast between visible and invisible, the image background and words, material image compared to its energetic meaning. This YIN and YANG, so to say, transferred into thinking and translated as real by your inner guide, that inner sacred light that guides the every human being. Bravo Gabriela, you are able to distinguish this light. What are you doing proves it!"

Sandu Napa, Teacher

"Gabriela, I want to thank you for your guidance and support in a very difficult time in my life. Your expert coaching, exercises, photo-coaching book and other related tools unstuck me—helping me to realize my true potential and talents and move forward. I'm now more focused, determined and confident about who I am, what is and is no longer important to me, what I want to achieve in my life and why. I feel well equipped to deal with anything that comes my way and ready to take it on!"

Janette Burke, Marketing/PR coach

~

"It is amazing how Gabriela, through her ingenious combination of coaching methods, guided me patiently and wisely to blowing up my limiting beliefs and leading to the biggest discovery of my life: the awareness of my inner force and its unlimited potential. Previously I was seeing life as being hard, but thanks to her mastery, my perspective shifted: I find it now as an incredibly exciting and enjoyable journey. I consider myself fortunate for the moment when our destinies crossed and grateful for every moment we have spent together."

Mihaela Fecioru, HR Specialist

~

"Gabriela is very intuitive and open-minded, which gives her great insight into understanding people on a deeper level. She has an excellent capacity to turn every situation into a self-discovery and learning opportunity, thus helping her clients come up with their own solutions. Moreover, by focusing on developing skills and teaching various techniques, she empowers and helps her clients learn how to be their own coach/therapist in the future. Overall, Gabriela is a great and inspiring coach!"

Melania Lumezanu, B.A Psych., M. ADS

I dedicate this book to ...

• *Those who didn't believe in my ability to help others through coaching. It's okay, there are other people who did (including myself). Disagreement has its benefits.*
• *Those who praise and support me while walking my path of heart. It counts more than you could ever imagine!*
And
• *Those who don't know me yet, but will be touched by this book: I'm so happy you found it!*

To all ... thank you!

Gabriela

≈

"The real man smiles in trouble, gathers strength from distress, and grows brave by reflection."

— THOMAS PAINE

WHAT IS PHOTO-COACHING?

Since I love nature and take lots of pictures, I occasionally noticed that some of them "speak" ... at least to me! :-)

In 2009, three years after I started my coaching practice, I began to feel frustrated that many people don't know what coaching is and what to expect from it. So I put together several "speaking" photos and the thoughts inspired by them, creating the first Photo-Coaching album as an invitation to self-reflection. I wanted to make *intangible coaching concepts* more *tangible* by combining visual elements with powerful coaching questions, and help people to apply them in their own life.

Encouraged by the profound mindset shifts that occurred in those who used the first Photo-Coaching album, in 2012 I created another one (about relationships). Soon after, life got in the way and I put this project aside.

Now I've been inspired to give it a new life as a series of published books. This way I can help more people while focusing on creating more books for the Photo-Coaching series (each designed around a specific theme).

As you probably noticed, I started to combine images and text even before Instagram was launched. :-)

Meeting With My Self:
Self-Coaching Questions That Invite Wisdom In

This first book in the Photo-Coaching series is about you!

I worked a lot on myself since 2006, and I can certainly see results. With this book, I invite you to a go for ... a meeting with your own Self! If you like what you get this time, you can come back to this book later on, anytime when you need more answers, inspiration, or motivation.

If you wonder why you need such meetings, let me assure you that your inner world is connected with what you see happening in your life right now. On each page of this book, you'll find a combination of photographs and questions that invite you to self-reflection, opening the door to a less explored place: your Inner World!

I hope this book and the next ones in this series will reveal more connections between your Inner and Outer Worlds.

Chapters 1 through 37 of this book will help you look at your situation from different perspectives, challenging your thinking, and helping you to see life from a more empowering point of view.

HOW TO USE THIS BOOK

Find a comfortable place, have a notebook handy and get ready to start your "journey".

Consider this book as a tool that facilitates the meeting between you with your Self. You will find below detailed instructions for the *first-time* use. I highly recommend that you go through the entire book (Chapters 1-37) the first time, to get used to its style and see what you can expect from it.

It is important to start with Chapter 1. Then, by going through all the chapters in order, you will get many ideas of possible actions. Jot them down, prioritize, and use Post-it notes as reminders to take those actions (or add them in your agenda). Without taking action, the desired changes might not occur!

Later on, come back to this book whenever you feel stressed, frustrated, have a problem or want to generate new ideas. At that time, start again with Chapter 1, then go quickly through the remaining chapters, stopping only at those which resonate with you in the moment—as they might "tell" you something new related to the new intention you're exploring. So the process is similar to the first-time use, although fewer chapters may be revisited. Depending on the situation, you might resonate with different chapters than before.

After exploring this Photo-Coaching book for the 1st or 2nd time, feel free to come up with other ways of using it. For example: focus on one chapter per day, or stay with a chapter until you take all the actions you came up with in the previous chapters.

Using this Photo-Coaching book for the **first time**

• *Start with Chapter 1*, where you are asked about your intention. Set one now, if you don't have it yet. It could be something you want to achieve or that bothers you (and you want to know what you can do about it), or simply a topic you want to explore. Write your intention in your notebook.

• *Clear your mind of any preconceived ideas*, and allow yourself to be curious (beginners' mind).

• *Go chapter by chapter and answer the questions* provided, or take time to reflect on each topic. Jot down the ideas you come up with based on each chapter's content. Also, write down the actions you could take to move you forward toward your intention.

• After you go through all chapters: *prioritize* the ideas and actions generated, from the most to least important.

• *Write the actions with a higher rank* on Post-it notes, give them *due dates*, and place them in areas you visit frequently. They will remind you to take those actions. If Post-it notes don't work for you, chose something else (it has to be something physical: agenda, phone calendar, etc). Believing that you will remember later might not work, because your list of ideas and actions will soon disappear from your focus when you get back to your busy life.

• *Take action!* Without taking the these actions, your good intentions won't move you forward!

• *Don't get discouraged* if your actions don't have any effect yet. It might take time until the desired results become visible.
• *Notice your progress* and *celebrate your successes*, even the small ones! (like getting the courage to complete an action)

Now grab your pen and notebook, and let's get started! :-)

~

Before we go further, **please set an intention!**
(something* that's important to you)

---

*A problem you want to solve or something you want to achieve.

~

Do you feel lost without a map?

If you're unhappy with your life,
chances are that your "map" is out of date.

What are you willing to do about it?

~

Our parents taught us what they knew about life,
as best they could.

Were they happy? Were they successful?
Did they follow their dreams?

If not*, do you want to continue to live your life based on the
same principles and beliefs?
Which ones are still useful for you now?
And which ones are not?

———

*This is not an invitation to turn against your parents. It is an invita-
tion to reflect on what principles and beliefs are still working for you
and which are not, so you can make the required adjustments.

~

When I was asked to write my epitaph,
it seemed weird at the beginning!
Then it made sense:
it pushed me to think about my life purpose.

What would you like to achieve* in this life?

Are you taking daily steps to get there?
Or are you a passenger, allowing someone else to drive your
car (life)?

---

*If you answered "I don't know", set an intention to find out what you want, and a due date. This way you'll set your mind to finding the answer. Coaching could really accelerate this process.

What's more important to you: the end result ...

... or the person you become in the process?

What are you willing to let go of …

… to welcome new things into your life?

… to be ready for success and happiness?

~

How much attention do you pay to where you go?

To what's happening in your life?

~

Some people are not afraid to get "wet"
when they want to achieve something.

Are you?

~

Which road would you like to travel:
1. The one crowded with worried, upset, unhappy people?
2. Your own path to success* and happiness?

The second path is not crowded, but what can you do differently to get there?

—

*According to your own definition of success.

~

On which side of the fence would you like to be?

1. Inside, governed by the limitations imposed by others?

2. Outside, free to explore the world and create the life you want?

～

How often do you ask someone for advice
or network with people around you?

How often do you pay attention to
your own intuition?

~

Do you have friends?

Do you connect with people who are going in the same direction
and supporting you?

OR

Do you surround yourself with people who keep you stuck or
drain your energy?

~

Do you allow the phantoms from the past to haunt you?

"I was told that…" , "My teacher said…",
"I was never good at…", etc.

Who can guarantee that those opinions are right?
Or that you haven't changed?

~

Am I a giant in this small world?

Not at all, it's just ... one point of view.

Do you feel overwhelmed?
Look at your problem from different perspectives.

What's good about your situation?

What can you learn from it?

What can you do differently next time?

Look for beauty and learn from everything,
even if it looks "dark" and "cold".

For example:

What's good about debt? It forces you to pay attention to your spending and investing, to understand the mindset of successful people, etc.

What's good about being single? You have the opportunity to spend more time with yourself, to (re)discover what's important for you, what you want, what's working or not …

~

How often do you put yourself on the edge: exploring or learning something new, getting out of your comfort zone?

Next time you will be more familiar with the situation, and you can expand your abilities even more!

Choose something new today*. What would you learn from it?

---

*Try a different perspective, do something in a new way, meet someone new, etc.

~

The water knows its intention
and is not afraid to jump, going with the flow.
Are you?

Are you ready to "jump" on a good opportunity, learn from it,
constantly adjusting your path to achieve your goals?

~

Is someone or something stopping you?
Think again!

How many times do you say "Yes",
when you really want to say "No"?

How often do you communicate what you want?
How focused are you on your intention?
Can you make quick decisions?

~

Got stuck?

Take route "66" instead! :-)
It might take you to a place where you will learn something new,
that will help you long term!

What alternate routes could be available?

~

How often do you quiet your mind?

Most people keep their mind busy:
worrying, analyzing problems, thinking ...
This could lead to a lack of ideas, to feeling tired, and hopeless.

Are you one of them?

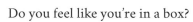

Do you feel like you're in a box?

Or stressed by the giants that surround you?

Step back and look from another perspective!

What are your strengths?
How can you make them work for you?

~

Some people don't like a rainy day, but I look
from a different angle …

… to find something …

… I can be grateful for!

What do you need to be grateful,
even on a "rainy" day?

How often do you reconnect ...

... with places that inspire you?

.

How can you become happier...

... without looking for another clown to cheer you up?

How focused are you on
what's really important to you?

The relationship itself is a separate entity.

How are you nurturing it?

What would you like to get out of it?

.

What can you learn from nature?

~

"Spring" (new opportunity) is coming.
Are you getting ready?

Do you pay attention to your physical strength, exercising and
eating properly?

What do you think about books?
Do you read any? What kind?

There are great books out there,
but just reading them won't move you forward!

What actions could be useful for you?

~

Are you seeing the world in terms of black and white,
good or bad?

The world just is! We choose how we see it.
What could help you to see both sides, and the nuances?
We always have options!

~

There are people who can transform even a wall
into something interesting.

Are you open to learn from the masters?

Now focus a few seconds on the next picture:

Did you notice a difference in how you feel, just by holding a different picture or thought in your mind?

On a daily basis, are you paying attention to what **thoughts** and **images** you are holding in your mind?

They could make you feel **happy** or **miserable**.

How often are you celebrating your successes,
no matter how big or small they are?

~

It takes 100 years to deposit 1 cm of
calcium carbonate on these stalagmites.

How patient are you?

How much do you believe in your intention, even when the
results are not yet visible?

~

What could you do to touch someone's soul?

A smile, acknowledging and encouraging people around you ...
might melt the ice!

And make you feel good at the same time.

~

Now please reconnect with the intention
I asked you to set at the beginning.

How useful was this presentation for your intention?

Did you allow yourself to get distracted
by the pictures and comments,
and forget about your intention?

If yes, how often does this happen in your life?

~

Still waiting for someone to show you the way?

To brainstorm solutions,
to challenge and keep you accountable?

AFTERWORD

~

Although I could add more chapters to this book, I was inspired to end it here. I will come back with other books in the Photo-Coaching series.

It seems natural to end the book with the question "Still waiting for someone to show you the way?" because a lot of people put aside their own dreams, and continue their life in the same direction — even if they don't get much satisfaction this way. Others would like to do something about their dreams, but they're waiting (for the right moment, the appropriate person to guide them) without realizing that — in fact — these will show up when they take themselves out of the waiting state by … taking the first step! Then take the another one, based on what they discover after the first step … and so on.

For me, life is like a journey that helps me know myself better, and such coaching questions are helpful in this process. That's why I created this book as a self-coaching guide, to help You … help Yourself!

Did you enjoy
Meeting With My Self: Self-Coaching Questions That Invite Wisdom In?

First of all, thank you for purchasing this book!

I am extremely grateful! I hope that it adds value and quality to your life, and that you'll come back to it when you need more ideas or feel stuck.

If you fond this book beneficial, may I ask you a big favor? Please leave a review for this book:

amazon.com/dp/B074QV64FQ

Meeting With My Self: Self-Coaching Questions that Invites the Wisdom In
by Gabriela Casineanu

Your feedback will help others make a more informed decision when considering buying this book. And who knows, maybe your review will also help others discover this book and change their lives!

It will also help me improve my writing craft and understand how the books in the Photo-Coaching series can be improved.

Let's build a better world together for all of us!

All the best,

Gabriela Casineanu

If you'd like to get notified when my next books will be published (Photo-Coaching or Introverts series):

GabrielaCasineanu.com/series

ABOUT THE AUTHOR

 Gabriela Casineanu has successfully navigated many life challenges and career transitions. She started her professional life in Engineering, later on adding coaching, entrepreneurship, art and writing ... continuing to explore life with the curiosity of a child!

She is a certified Professional Coach by the International Coach Federation (2008), and was trained by two prestigious coaching training schools: CTI (Co-Active Coaching, 2006) and CRR Global (Organization & Relationship Systems Coaching, 2009).

With a daily meditation practice and a passion for self-discovery, she relies on intuition to guide her next steps.

Reflecting on her own path, Gabriela Casineanu considers life as a self-discovery journey. She'll elaborate more on this in her next books. :-)

GabrielaCasineanu.com
gabriela.casineanu@gmail.com

Instagram: ThoughtsDesigner
Facebook: GC.ThoughtsDesigner
Twitter: @thoughtdesigner
LinkedIn: gabrielacasineanu

ALSO BY GABRIELA CASINEANU

• *Introverts: Leverage Your Strengths for an Effective Job Search*

A comprehensive book, based on over 10 years experience in of coaching and employment counseling, showing how the quiet individuals can use their strengths to land their desired job and build a rewarding career:

amazon.com/dp/B0732L97DL

Available also on iTunes, Kobo, Nook, Audible

• **To receive notifications** about Gabriela's upcoming books in **Introverts** and **Photo-Coaching series**:

http://www.gabrielacasineanu.com/series

• **For business owners**

Do you find yourself repeating the same information to each new client? Do you like how this book transforms non-tangible concepts into more tangible and easy to understand information?

Contact Gabriela to discuss how to "package" your information in a booklet that is easy for your clients to understand. In this way you could free up your time for the other important business tasks leading to business growth.

• **Coaching, Workshops, Webinars:** GabrielaCasineanu.com

ACKNOWLEDGMENTS

Many thanks to …

… my family, friends, coaching clients and readers who openly shared their experience of using the content of this book;

… my fellow authors, for their encouragement and support;

… the coaching schools that helped me discover the meaning and power of self-growth, leading to opening my heart to spirituality.

Printed in Great Britain
by Amazon

41203926R00062